Table of Contents

PEPPERMINT LANE QUILT FEATURES THE VINTAGE HOLIDAY COLLECTION BY BONNIE & CAMILLE FOR MODA FABRICS.

67 ½" x 81 ½"

Month One — Gingerbread Boy Blocks

55162-18	55167-12	55161-13	55162-15
½ yard	14" x 20"	14" x 20"	10" x 10"

Month Two — Candy Cottage Block

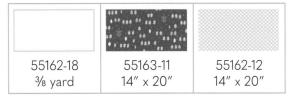

55162-18	55163-11	55162-12	55168-14	55167-11	55162-18M	55164-16
10" x 15"	14" x 20"	12" x 20"	10" x 10"	10" x 10"	10" x 10"	5" x 15"

Month Three — Star Studded Blocks

55162-18	55163-11	55162-12
⅜ yard	14" x 20"	14" x 20"

Month Four — Vintage Ornaments Block

55162-18	55161-15	55166-16	55167-11	55161-18	55166-14	55168-18M
½ yard	10" x 10"	10" x 10"	10" x 10"	10" x 10"	10" x 10"	10" x 15"

Month Five — Deck the Halls Blocks

55162-18	55162-16	55169-11
¼ yard	12" x 20"	10" x 10"

Month Six — Trim the Tree Block

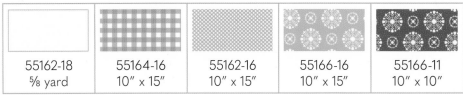

55162-18	55164-16	55162-16	55166-16	55166-11
⅝ yard	10" x 15"	10" x 15"	10" x 15"	10" x 10"

Month Seven — Holiday Homecoming Block

55162-18	55164-16	55161-13	55166-16	55162-15
18" x 20"	12" x 20"	12" x 20"	12" x 20"	10" x 15"

Month Eight — Santa's Stocking Blocks

55162-18	55166-11	55161-15	55168-18M	55162-18M
12" x 20"	12" x 20"	12" x 20"	10" x 10"	10" x 20"

Month Nine — Peppermint Stick Blocks

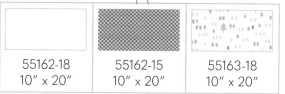

55162-18	55162-15	55163-18
10" x 20"	10" x 20"	10" x 20"

Month Ten — Season of Giving Block

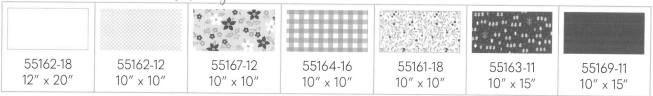

55162-18	55162-12	55167-12	55164-16	55161-18	55163-11	55169-11
12" x 20"	10" x 10"	10" x 10"	10" x 10"	10" x 10"	10" x 15"	10" x 15"

Month Eleven — Cozy Cocoa Block

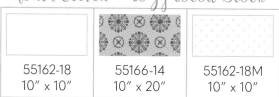

55162-18	55166-14	55162-18M
10" x 10"	10" x 20"	10" x 10"

Month Twelve — Finishing

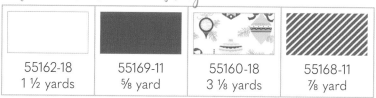

55162-18	55169-11	55160-18	55168-11
1 ½ yards	⅝ yard	3 ⅛ yards	⅞ yard

Backing

55167-18
5 ⅛ yards

Unfinished size: 11 ½" x 14 ½"
Make two total

Cutting Instructions:

FROM THE BACKGROUND FABRIC CUT:

	4 - 4 ⅛" x 4 ¼" rectangles	A
	4 - 3 ¾" squares	B
	4 - 3 ½" x 3 ¾" rectangles	C
	4 - 2 ½" squares	D
	2 - 2" x 11 ½" rectangles	E
	20 - 1 ½" squares	F

FROM EACH GINGERBREAD BOY FABRIC CUT:

	1 - 4 ¼" square	G
	2 - 3 ¾" x 6" rectangles	H
	1 - 3 ¾" square	I
	2 - 3" x 4 ¾" rectangles	J
	2 - 2 ¼" x 3 ½" rectangles	K
	1 - 1 ½" square	L

FROM THE BOWTIES AND BUTTONS FABRIC CUT:

	1 - 3 ¾" square	M
	4 - 1 ½" squares	N

Piecing Instructions:

Draw a diagonal line on the wrong side of the Fabric F squares.

With right sides facing, layer a Fabric F square on one corner of a Fabric G square.

Stitch on the drawn line and trim ¼" away from the seam.

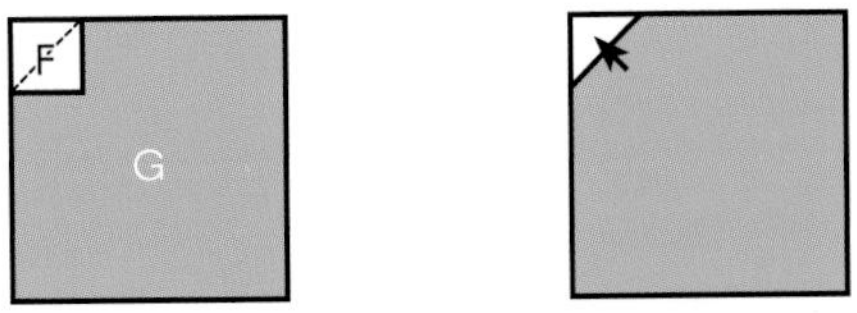

Repeat on the remaining corners.

Gingerbread Boy Head Unit should measure 4 ¼" x 4 ¼".

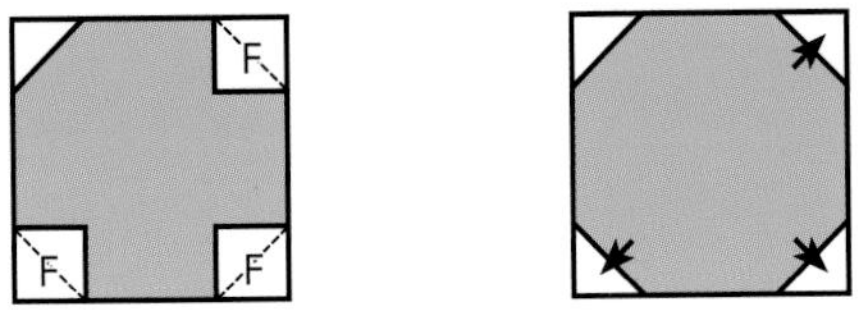

Make one from each Gingerbread Boy Fabric.

Make two total.

With right sides facing, layer a Fabric F square on the top left corner of a Fabric J rectangle.

Stitch on the drawn line and trim ¼" away from the seam.

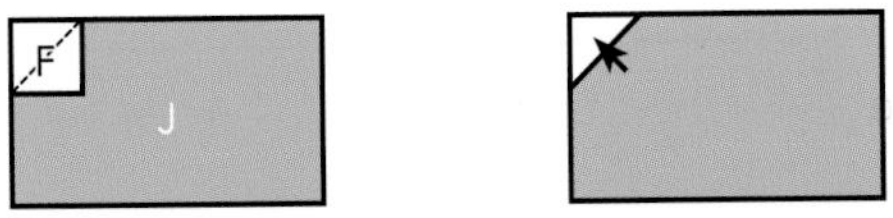

Repeat on the bottom left corner.

Gingerbread Boy Arm Unit should measure 3" x 4 ¾".

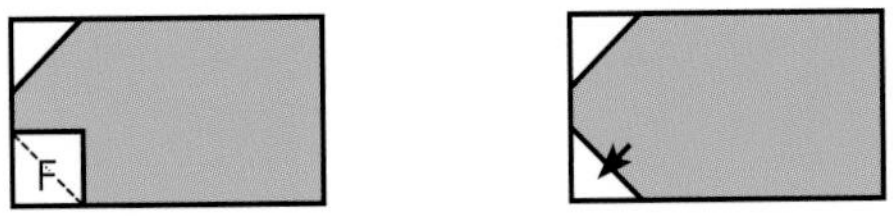

Make two from each Gingerbread Boy Fabric.

Make four total.

Cut the Fabric I squares on the diagonal twice.

Make four from each Gingerbread Boy Fabric.
Make eight total.

Cut the Fabric M square on the diagonal twice.

Make four.

Assemble Unit using matching fabric.
Bowtie Unit should measure 3" x 3".

Make one from each Gingerbread Boy Fabric.
Make two total.
You will not use all Fabric I triangles.

Draw a diagonal line on the wrong side of the Fabric B squares and Fabric D squares.

With right sides facing, layer a Fabric B square on the left end of a Fabric H rectangle.

Stitch on the drawn line and trim ¼" away from the seam.

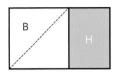 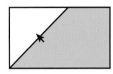

Repeat on the bottom left corner with a Fabric F square and the bottom right corner with a Fabric D square.

Left Gingerbread Boy Leg Unit should measure 3 ¾" x 6".

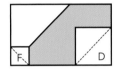 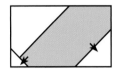

Make one from each Gingerbread Boy Fabric.
Make two total.

With right sides facing, layer a Fabric B square on the right end of a Fabric H rectangle.

Stitch on the drawn line and trim ¼" away from the seam.

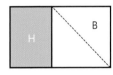 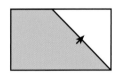

Repeat on the bottom left corner with a Fabric D square and the bottom right corner with a Fabric F square.

Right Gingerbread Boy Leg Unit should measure 3 ¾" x 6".

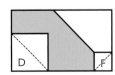 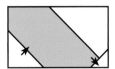

Make one from each Gingerbread Boy Fabric.
Make two total.

Assemble Unit using matching fabric.

Gingerbread Boy Unit should measure 3 ½" x 11 ½".

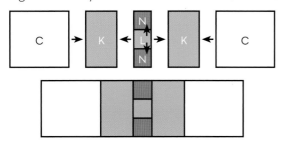

Make one from each Gingerbread Boy Fabric.

Make two total.

Assemble Block using matching fabric.

Gingerbread Boy Block should measure 11 ½" x 14 ½".

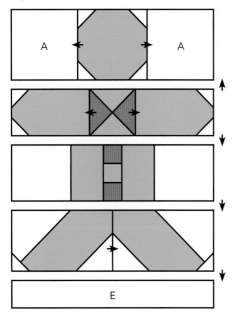

Make one from each Gingerbread Boy Fabric.

Make two total.

Unfinished size: 11 ½" x 14 ½"
Make one

Cutting Instructions:

FROM THE BACKGROUND FABRIC CUT:		
	2 - 3 ½" squares	A
	1 - 2" x 7" rectangle	B
	1 - 2" x 3 ½" rectangle	C
	2 - 1" x 8" rectangles	D

FROM THE ROOF AND CHIMNEY FABRIC CUT:		
	1 - 3 ½" x 11 ½" rectangle	E
	1 - 2" square	F
	1 - 1 ½" x 4" rectangle	G
	7 - 1" x 2" rectangles	H
	4 - 1" x 1 ½" rectangles	I

FROM THE COTTAGE SIDING FABRIC CUT:		
	1 - 3" x 7" rectangle	J
	2 - 2 ½" x 4" rectangles	K
	1 - 2" x 8" rectangle	L
	1 - 2" x 2 ½" rectangle	M
	2 - 2" squares	N
	2 - 1 ½" x 2 ½" rectangles	O
	2 - 1 ½" squares	P
	22 - 1" squares	Q

FROM THE DOOR FABRIC CUT:		
	1 - 3" x 4" rectangle	R
	4 - 1" squares	S

FROM THE RED WINDOW FABRIC CUT:		
	1 - 3 ¼" square	T

FROM THE WHITE WINDOW FABRIC CUT:		
	1 - 3 ¼" square	U

FROM THE GRASS FABRIC CUT:		
	1 - 2" x 11 ½" rectangle	V

Piecing Instructions:

Draw a diagonal line on the wrong side of the Fabric A squares.

With right sides facing, layer a Fabric A square on one end of the Fabric E rectangle.

Stitch on the drawn line and trim ¼" away from the seam.

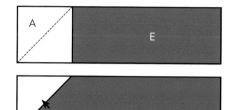

Repeat on the opposite end.

Top Roof Unit should measure 3 ½" x 11 ½".

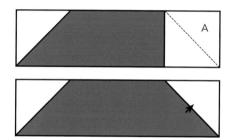

Make one.

Draw a diagonal line on the wrong side of the Fabric Q squares.

With right sides facing, layer a Fabric Q square on the right end of a Fabric I rectangle.

Stitch on the drawn line and trim ¼" away from the seam.

Left Scallop Roof Unit should measure 1" x 1 ½".

Make one.

With right sides facing, layer a Fabric Q square on one end of a Fabric H rectangle.

Stitch on the drawn line and trim ¼" away from the seam.

Repeat on the opposite end.

Middle Scallop Roof Unit should measure 1" x 2".

Make six.

With right sides facing, layer a Fabric Q square on the left end of a Fabric I rectangle.

Stitch on the drawn line and trim ¼" away from the seam.

Right Scallop Roof Unit should measure 1" x 1 ½".

Make one.

Assemble Unit.

Scallop Roof Unit should measure 1" x 11 ½".

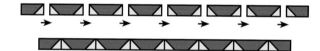

Make one.

Draw a diagonal line on the wrong side of the Fabric P squares.

With right sides facing, layer a Fabric P square on one end of the Fabric G rectangle.

Stitch on the drawn line and trim ¼" away from the seam.

Repeat on the opposite end.

Partial Awning Unit should measure 1 ½" x 4".

Make one.

Draw a diagonal line on the wrong side of the Fabric S squares.

With right sides facing, layer a Fabric S square on the right end of a Fabric I rectangle.

Stitch on the drawn line and trim ¼" away from the seam.

Left Scallop Awning Unit should measure 1" x 1 ½".

Make one.

With right sides facing, layer a Fabric S square on one end of the remaining Fabric H rectangle.

Stitch on the drawn line and trim ¼" away from the seam.

Repeat on the opposite end.

Middle Scallop Awning Unit should measure 1" x 2".

Make one.

With right sides facing, layer a Fabric S square on the left end of a Fabric I rectangle.

Stitch on the drawn line and trim ¼" away from the seam.

Right Scallop Awning Unit should measure 1" x 1 ½".

Make one.

Assemble Unit.

Awning Unit should measure 2" x 4".

Make one.

Assemble Unit.

Left Cottage Unit should measure 7" x 8".

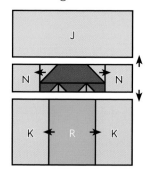   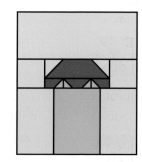

Make one.

Cut the Fabric T square on the diagonal twice.

Make four.

Cut the Fabric U square on the diagonal twice.

Make four.

Assemble Unit.

Partial Window Unit should measure 2 ½" x 2 ½".

Make two.

With right sides facing, layer a Fabric Q square on one corner of a Partial Window Unit.

Stitch on the drawn line and trim ¼" away from the seam.

Repeat on the remaining corners.

Window Unit should measure 2 ½" x 2 ½".

Make two.

Assemble Unit. Pay close attention to direction of Window Units.

Candy Cottage Unit should measure 8" x 11 ½".

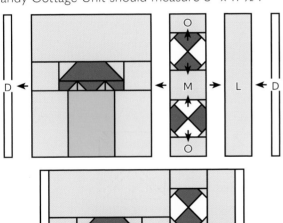

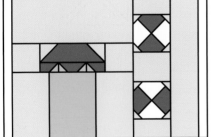

Make one.

Assemble Block.

Candy Cottage Block should measure 11 ½" x 14 ½".

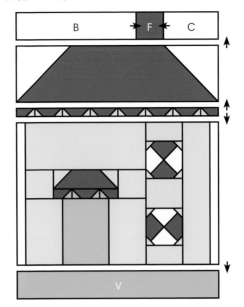

Make one.

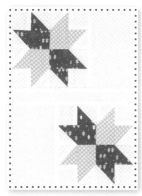

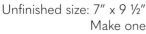

Unfinished size: 7" x 9 ½"
Make one

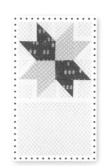

Unfinished size: 4 ½" x 7 ½"
Make one

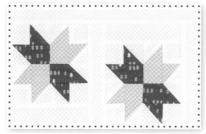

Unfinished size: 6 ½" x 10 ½"
Make two

Piecing Instructions:

Draw a diagonal line on the wrong side of the Fabric C squares.

With right sides facing, layer a Fabric C square with a Fabric J square.

Stitch ¼" from each side of the drawn line.

Cut apart on the marked line.

Red Half Square Triangle Unit should measure 1 ½" x 1 ½".

Make fourteen.

Draw a diagonal line on the wrong side of the Fabric I squares.

With right sides facing, layer a Fabric I square on the left end of a Fabric K rectangle.

Stitch on the drawn line and trim ¼" away from the seam.

Partial Red Star Unit should measure 1 ½" x 2 ½".

Make fourteen.

Assemble Unit.

Red Star Unit should measure 2 ½" x 2 ½".

Make fourteen.

With right sides facing, layer a Fabric C square with a Fabric L square.

Stitch ¼" from each side of the drawn line.

Cut apart on the marked line.

Blue Half Square Triangle Unit should measure 1 ½" x 1 ½".

Make fourteen.

Cutting Instructions:

FROM THE BACKGROUND FABRIC CUT:		
1 - 3 ½" x 4 ½" rectangle	A
2 - 3" x 4 ½" rectangles	B
14 - 1 ⅞" squares	C
2 - 1 ½" x 10 ½" rectangles	D
1 - 1 ½" x 7" rectangle	E
4 - 1 ½" x 5 ½" rectangles	F
4 - 1 ½" x 4 ½" rectangles	G
28 - 1 ½" squares	H
28 - 1 ½" squares	I

FROM THE RED STAR POINTS FABRIC CUT:		
7 - 1 ⅞" squares	J
14 - 1 ½" x 2 ½" rectangles	K

FROM THE BLUE STAR POINTS FABRIC CUT:		
7 - 1 ⅞" squares	L
14 - 1 ½" x 2 ½" rectangles	M

With right sides facing, layer a Fabric I square on the bottom end of a Fabric M rectangle.

Stitch on the drawn line and trim ¼" away from the seam.

Partial Blue Star Unit should measure 1 ½" x 2 ½".

Make fourteen.

Assemble Unit.

Blue Star Unit should measure 2 ½" x 2 ½".

Make fourteen.

Assemble Unit.

Star Unit should measure 4 ½" x 4 ½".

Make seven.

Assemble Block.

Star Studded Block One should measure 7" x 9 ½".

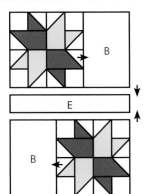 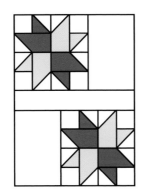

Make one.

Assemble Unit.

Star Studded Unit should measure 4 ½" x 5 ½".

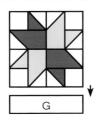 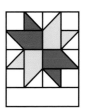

Make four.

Assemble Block.

Star Studded Block Two should measure 6 ½" x 10 ½".

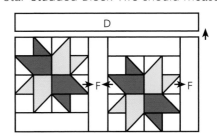

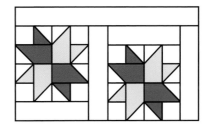

Make two.

Assemble Block.

Star Studded Block Three should measure 4 ½" x 7 ½".

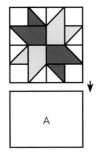 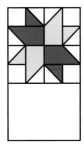

Make one.

Unfinished size: 9 ½" x 29"

Make one

Cutting Instructions:

FROM THE BACKGROUND FABRIC CUT:		
	5 - 2 ½" x 5" rectangles	A
	10 - 2 ¼" x 2 ½" rectangles	B
	20 - 1 ¾" squares	C
	6 - 1 ½" x 9 ½" rectangles	D
	40 - 1 ½" squares	E
	10 - 1 ¼" x 2" rectangles	F

FROM EACH ORNAMENT FABRIC CUT:		
	9 - 2" squares	G

FROM THE ORNAMENT HANGER FABRIC CUT:		
	5 - 1 ¼" x 2" rectangles	H
	5 - 1" x 2 ¼" rectangles	I

Piecing Instructions:

Draw a diagonal line on the wrong side of the Fabric C squares.

With right sides facing, layer a Fabric C square on the top left corner of a Fabric G square.

Stitch on the drawn line and trim ¼" away from the seam.

Corner Ornament Unit should measure 2" x 2".

Make four from each Ornament Fabric.

Make twenty total.

Draw a diagonal line on the wrong side of the Fabric E squares.

With right sides facing, layer a Fabric E square on the bottom left corner of a Fabric G square.

Stitch on the drawn line and trim ¼" away from the seam.

Repeat on the bottom right corner.

Middle Ornament Unit should measure 2" x 2".

Make four from each Ornament Fabric.

Make twenty total.

Assemble Unit using matching fabric.

Partial Ornament Unit should measure 5" x 5".

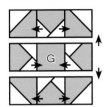 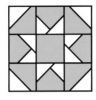

Make one from each Ornament Fabric.

Make five total.

Assemble Unit.

Ornament Unit should measure 5" x 7 ½".

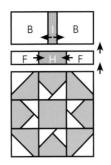 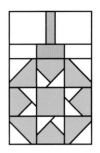

Make one from each Ornament Fabric.

Make five total.

Assemble Block.

Vintage Ornaments Block should measure 9 ½" x 29".

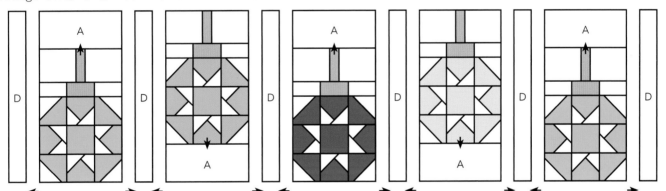

Make one.

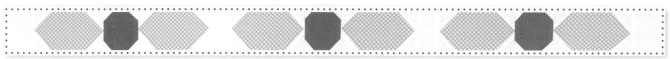

Unfinished size: 2 ½" x 35 ½"
Make one

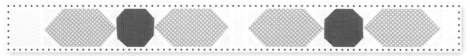

Unfinished size: 2 ½" x 24 ½"
Make one

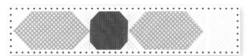

Unfinished size: 2 ½" x 12 ½"
Make one

Piecing Instructions:

Draw a diagonal line on the wrong side of the Fabric D squares.

With right sides facing, layer a Fabric D square on one corner of a Fabric F rectangle.

Stitch on the drawn line and trim ¼" away from the seam.

Repeat on the remaining corners.

Leaf Unit should measure 2 ½" x 4 ½".

Make twelve.

Cutting Instructions:

FROM THE BACKGROUND FABRIC CUT:		
	2 - 2 ½" squares	A
	4 - 1 ¾" x 2 ½" rectangles	B
	2 - 1 ½" x 2 ½" rectangles	C
	48 - 1 ½" squares	D
	24 - 1" squares	E
FROM THE LEAF FABRIC CUT:		
	12 - 2 ½" x 4 ½" rectangles	F
FROM THE BERRY FABRIC CUT:		
	6 - 2 ½" squares	G

Draw a diagonal line on the wrong side of the Fabric E squares.

With right sides facing, layer a Fabric E square on one corner of a Fabric G square.

Stitch on the drawn line and trim ¼" away from the seam.

Repeat on the remaining corners.

Berry Unit should measure 2 ½" x 2 ½".

Make six.

Assemble Unit.

Holly Unit should measure 2 ½″ x 10 ½″.

Make six.

Assemble Block.

Deck the Halls Block One should measure 2 ½″ x 35 ½″.

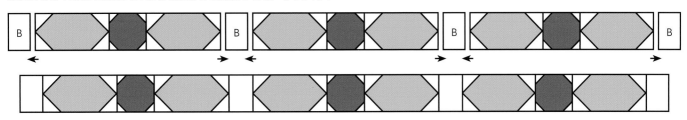

Make one.

Assemble Block.

Deck the Halls Block Two should measure 2 ½″ x 24 ½″.

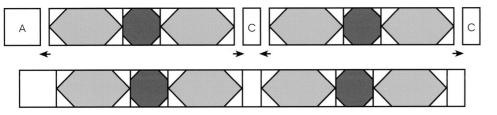

Make one.

Assemble Block.

Deck the Halls Block Three should measure 2 ½″ x 12 ½″.

Make one.

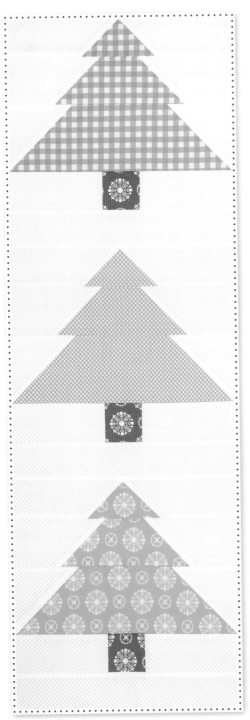

Unfinished size: 12 ½" x 36 ½"
Make one

Cutting Instructions:

FROM THE BACKGROUND FABRIC CUT:	
6 - 4" squares	A
6 - 3" x 5 ½" rectangles	B
3 - 2 ½" x 12 ½" rectangles	C
6 - 2 ½" x 6 ½" rectangles	D
6 - 2 ½" x 5 ½" rectangles	E

FROM EACH CHRISTMAS TREE FABRIC CUT:	
1 - 4" x 12 ½" rectangle	F
1 - 3" x 7 ½" rectangle	G
1 - 2 ½" x 4 ½" rectangle	H

FROM THE TREE TRUNK FABRIC CUT:	
3 - 2 ½" squares	I

Piecing Instructions:

On the wrong side of the Fabric H rectangles, mark a dot 2 ½" up from the bottom right corner. Draw a line from the bottom left corner to the dot.

With right sides facing, layer the Fabric H rectangle with a Fabric D rectangle. Stitch on the drawn line and trim ¼" away from the seam.

Partial Top Christmas Tree Unit should measure 2 ½" x 8 ½".

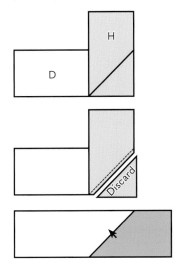

Make one from each Christmas Tree Fabric.

Make three total.

On the wrong side of the remaining Fabric D rectangles, mark a dot 2 ½" down from the top right corner. Draw a line from the top left corner to the dot.

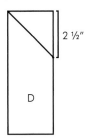

With right sides facing, layer a marked Fabric D rectangle with a Partial Top Christmas Tree Unit. Stitch on the drawn line and trim ¼" away from the seam.

Top Christmas Tree Unit should measure 2 ½" x 12 ½".

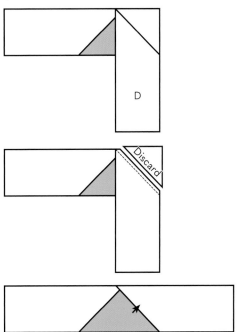

Make one from each Christmas Tree Fabric.

Make three total.

On the wrong side of the Fabric G rectangles, mark a dot 3" up from the bottom right corner. Draw a line from the bottom left corner to the dot.

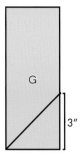

With right sides facing, layer the Fabric G rectangle with a Fabric B rectangle. Stitch on the drawn line and trim ¼" away from the seam.

Partial Middle Christmas Tree Unit should measure 3" x 10".

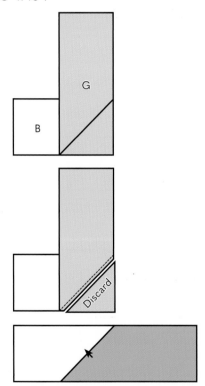

Make one from each Christmas Tree Fabric.

Make three total.

On the wrong side of the remaining Fabric B rectangles, mark a dot 3" down from the top right corner. Draw a line from the top left corner to the dot.

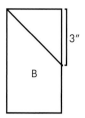

With right sides facing, layer a marked Fabric B rectangle with a Partial Middle Christmas Tree Unit. Stitch on the drawn line and trim ¼" away from the seam.

Middle Christmas Tree Unit should measure 3" x 12 ½".

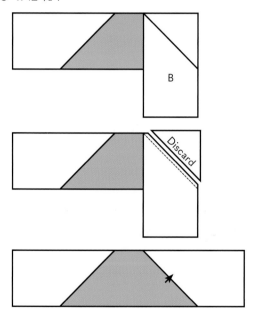

Make one from each Christmas Tree Fabric.

Make three total.

Draw a diagonal line on the wrong side of the Fabric A squares.

With right sides facing, layer a Fabric A square on one end of a Fabric F rectangle.

Stitch on the drawn line and trim ¼" away from the seam.

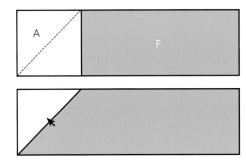

Repeat on the opposite end.

Bottom Christmas Tree Unit should measure 4" x 12 ½".

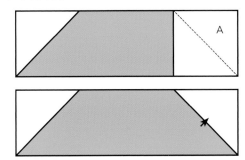

Make one from each Christmas Tree Fabric.

Make three total.

Assemble Unit.

Tree Trunk Unit should measure 2 ½" x 12 ½".

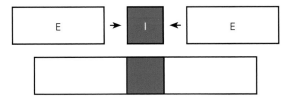

Make three.

Assemble Block.

Trim the Tree Block should measure 12 ½" x 36 ½".

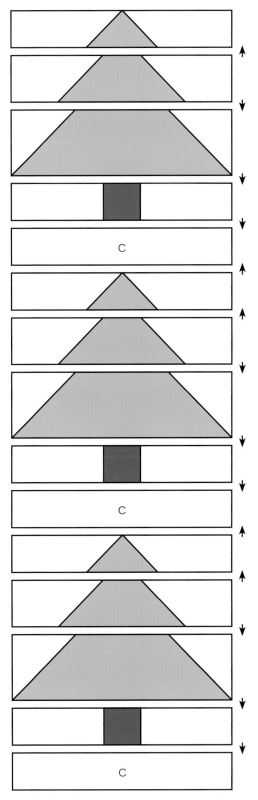

Make one.

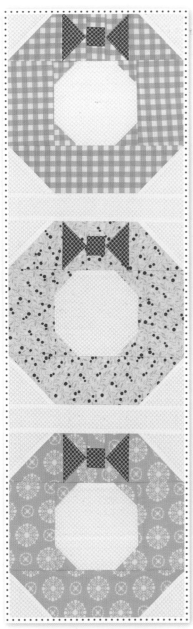

Unfinished size: 10" x 32"
Make one

Cutting Instructions:

FROM THE BACKGROUND FABRIC CUT:	
3 - 5" squares	A
12 - 3" squares	B
2 - 2" x 10" rectangles	C

FROM EACH WREATH FABRIC CUT:	
1 - 3" x 10" rectangle	D
2 - 3" x 5" rectangles	E
2 - 3" x 3 ½" rectangles	F
8 - 1 ¾" squares	G
2 - 1 ¼" x 1 ½" rectangles	H

FROM THE BOW FABRIC CUT:	
6 - 1 ¾" x 3" rectangles	I
3 - 1 ½" squares	J

Piecing Instructions:

Draw a diagonal line on the wrong side of the Fabric B squares.

With right sides facing, layer a Fabric B square on the left end of a Fabric F rectangle.

Stitch on the drawn line and trim ¼" away from the seam.

Top Left Wreath Unit should measure 3" x 3 ½".

Make one from each Wreath Fabric.

Make three total.

Draw a diagonal line on the wrong side of the Fabric G squares.

With right sides facing, layer a Fabric G square on the top end of a Fabric I rectangle.

Stitch on the drawn line and trim ¼" away from the seam.

Repeat on the bottom end using matching fabric.

Flying Geese Unit should measure 1 ¾" x 3".

Make two from each Wreath Fabric.

Make six total.

With right sides facing, layer a Fabric B square on the right end of a Fabric F rectangle.

Stitch on the drawn line and trim ¼" away from the seam.

Top Right Wreath Unit should measure 3" x 3 ½".

Make one from each Wreath Fabric.

Make three total.

Assemble Unit using matching fabric.

Top Wreath Unit should measure 3" x 10".

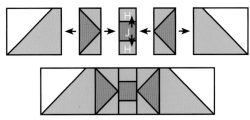

Make one from each Wreath Fabric.

Make three total.

With right sides facing, layer a Fabric G square on one corner of a Fabric A square.

Stitch on the drawn line and trim ¼" away from the seam.

Repeat on the remaining corners using matching fabric.

Center Wreath Unit should measure 5" x 5".

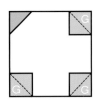

Make one from each Wreath Fabric.

Make three total.

Assemble Unit using matching fabric.

Middle Wreath Unit should measure 5" x 10".

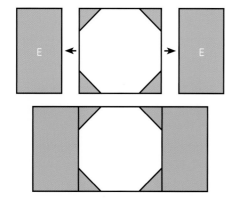

Make one from each Wreath Fabric.

Make three total.

With right sides facing, layer a Fabric B square on one end of a Fabric D rectangle.

Stitch on the drawn line and trim ¼" away from the seam.

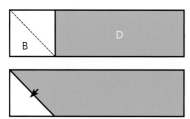

Repeat on the opposite end.

Bottom Wreath Unit should measure 3" x 10".

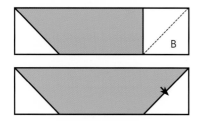

Make one from each Wreath Fabric.

Make three total.

Assemble Block.

Holiday Homecoming Block should measure 10" x 32".

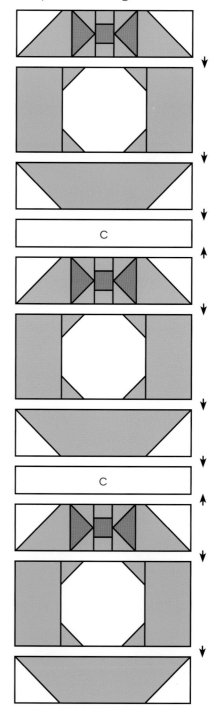

Make one.

Unfinished size: 10 ½" x 12 ½"
Make two total

Piecing Instructions:

Draw a diagonal line on the wrong side of the Fabric L squares.

With right sides facing, layer a Fabric L square on one end of a Fabric H rectangle.

Stitch on the drawn line and trim ¼" away from the seam.

Repeat on the opposite end.

Dark Flying Geese Unit should measure 1 ½" x 2 ½".

Make six from each Stocking Fabric.

Make twelve total.

 ————————————————

Draw a diagonal line on the wrong side of the Fabric I squares.

With right sides facing, layer a Fabric I square on one end of a Fabric K rectangle.

Stitch on the drawn line and trim ¼" away from the seam.

Repeat on the opposite end using matching fabric.

Light Flying Geese Unit should measure 1 ½" x 2 ½".

Make six from each Stocking Fabric.

Make twelve total.

Cutting Instructions:

FROM THE BACKGROUND FABRIC CUT:

2 - 3 ½" x 5 ½" rectangles	A
2 - 3" squares	B
2 - 2 ½" x 3" rectangles	C
4 - 2" squares	D
2 - 1 ½" x 10" rectangles	E

FROM EACH STOCKING FABRIC CUT:

1 - 5" x 9 ½" rectangle	F
1 - 1 ½" x 6 ½" rectangle	G
6 - 1 ½" x 2 ½" rectangles	H
12 - 1 ½" squares	I

FROM THE CUFF FABRIC CUT:

2 - 3" x 8 ½" rectangles	J

FROM THE CHEVRON STRIPE FABRIC CUT:

12 - 1 ½" x 2 ½" rectangles	K
24 - 1 ½" squares	L

Assemble Unit using matching fabric.

Chevron Stocking Unit should measure 5 ½" x 6 ½".

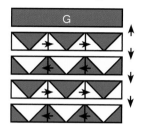
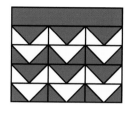

Make one from each Stocking Fabric.

Make two total.

Draw a diagonal line on the wrong side of the Fabric B squares and Fabric D squares.

With right sides facing, layer a Fabric B square on the bottom right corner of a Fabric F rectangle.

Stitch on the drawn line and trim ¼" away from the seam.

Repeat on the top left and bottom left corners with Fabric D squares.

Bottom Stocking Unit should measure 5" x 9 ½".

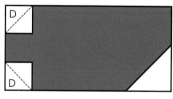

Make one from each Stocking Fabric.

Make two total.

Assemble Unit using matching fabric.

Stocking Unit should measure 9 ½" x 10".

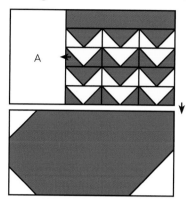

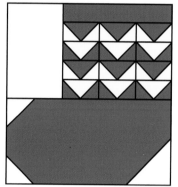

Make one from each Stocking Fabric.

Make two total.

Assemble Block.

Santa's Stocking Block should measure 10 ½" x 12 ½".

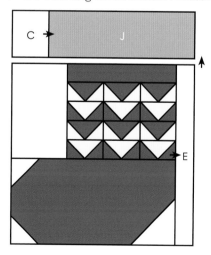

Make one from each Stocking Fabric.

Make two total.

Unfinished size: 3 ½" x 5 ½"
Make five

Cutting Instructions:

FROM THE BACKGROUND FABRIC CUT:		
	5 - 2 ½" x 3 ½" rectangles	A
	3 - 1 ⅞" squares	B
	5 - 1 ½" squares	C
	5 - 1 ½" squares	D

FROM THE RED CANDY CANE FABRIC CUT:		
	21 - 1 ⅞" squares	E

FROM THE WHITE CANDY CANE FABRIC CUT:		
	18 - 1 ⅞" squares	F

Piecing Instructions:

Draw a diagonal line on the wrong side of the Fabric F squares.

With right sides facing, layer a Fabric F square with a Fabric E square.

Stitch ¼" from each side of the drawn line.

Cut apart on the marked line.

Peppermint Stick Half Square Triangle Unit should measure 1 ½" x 1 ½".

Make thirty-six.

You will not use all Units.

Draw a diagonal line on the wrong side of the Fabric B squares.

With right sides facing, layer a Fabric B square with a Fabric E square.

Stitch ¼" from each side of the drawn line.

Cut apart on the marked line.

Background Half Square Triangle Unit should measure 1 ½" x 1 ½".

Make six.

You will not use all Units.

Draw a diagonal line on the wrong side of the Fabric C squares.

With right sides facing, layer a Fabric C square with a Peppermint Stick Half Square Triangle Unit.

Pay close attention to unit placement.

Stitch on the drawn line and trim ¼" away from the seam.

Top Left Peppermint Stick Unit should measure 1 ½" x 1 ½".

Make five.

Assemble Unit.

Top Peppermint Stick Unit should measure
2 ½" x 3 ½".

Make five.

Assemble Unit.

Bottom Peppermint Stick Unit should measure
3 ½" x 3 ½".

Make five.

Assemble Block.

Peppermint Stick Block should measure 3 ½" x 5 ½".

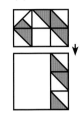 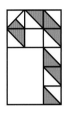

Make five.

Unfinished size: 9 ½" x 24 ½"
Make one

Cutting Instructions:

FROM THE BACKGROUND FABRIC CUT:

	4 - 3 ⅜" squares	A
	4 - 1 ½" x 9 ½" rectangles	B
	2 - 1 ½" x 5 ½" rectangles	C

FROM EACH BLUE PRESENT FABRIC CUT:

	4 - 2 ¾" x 3 ½" rectangles	D

FROM EACH GREEN PRESENT FABRIC CUT:

	4 - 2 ¾" x 3" rectangles	E

FROM THE BOW FABRIC CUT:

	4 - 3 ⅜" squares	F
	8 - 1 ½" squares	G

FROM THE RIBBON FABRIC CUT:

	4 - 1" x 5 ½" rectangles	H
	4 - 1" x 3 ½" rectangles	I
	4 - 1" x 3" rectangles	J

Piecing Instructions:

Draw a diagonal line on the wrong side of the Fabric A squares.

With right sides facing, layer a Fabric A square with a Fabric F square.

Stitch ¼" from each side of the drawn line.

Cut apart on the marked line.

Half Square Triangle Unit should measure 3" x 3".

Make eight.

Draw a diagonal line on the wrong side of the Fabric G squares.

With right sides facing, layer a Fabric G square on the bottom right corner of a Half Square Triangle Unit.

Pay close attention to unit placement.

Stitch on the drawn line and trim ¼" away from the seam.

Left Bow Unit should measure 3" x 3".

Make four.

With right sides facing, layer a Fabric G square on the bottom left corner of a Half Square Triangle Unit.

Pay close attention to unit placement.

Stitch on the drawn line and trim ¼" away from the seam.

Right Bow Unit should measure 3" x 3".

Make four.

Assemble Unit using matching fabric.

Blue Present Unit should measure 5 ½" x 9 ½".

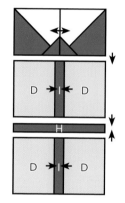 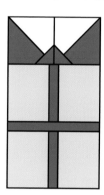

Make one from each Blue Present Fabric.

Make two total.

Assemble Unit using matching fabric.

Green Present Unit should measure 5 ½" x 9 ½".

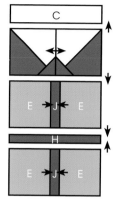 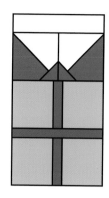

Make one from each Green Present Fabric.

Make two total.

Assemble Block.

Season of Giving Block should measure 9 ½" x 24 ½".

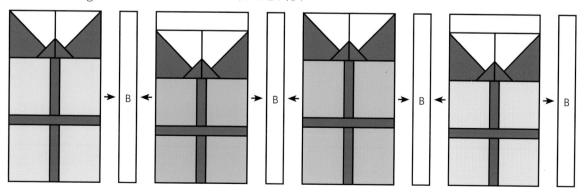

Make one.

Unfinished size: 7 ½" x 7 ½"
Make one

Piecing Instructions:

Draw a diagonal line on the wrong side of the Fabric I squares.

With right sides facing, layer a Fabric I square on the bottom left corner of a Fabric E rectangle.

Stitch on the drawn line and trim ¼" away from the seam.

Repeat on the bottom right corner.

Star Point Unit should measure 2" x 2 ¼".

Make four.

Assemble Unit.

Cozy Cocoa Unit should measure 5 ½" x 7 ½".

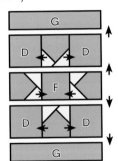 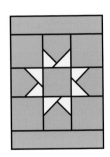

Make one.

Cutting Instructions:

FROM THE BACKGROUND FABRIC CUT:		
	1 - 2 ½" square	A
	2 - 1 ½" x 2 ½" rectangles	B
	2 - 1 ½" squares	C

FROM THE COZY COCOA FABRIC CUT:		
	4 - 2 ¼" squares	D
	4 - 2" x 2 ¼" rectangles	E
	1 - 2" square	F
	2 - 1 ½" x 5 ½" rectangles	G
	3 - 1 ½" x 2 ½" rectangles	H

FROM THE STAR POINT FABRIC CUT:		
	8 - 1 ½" squares	I

Draw a diagonal line on the wrong side of the Fabric C squares.

With right sides facing, layer a Fabric C square on the right end of a Fabric H rectangle.

Stitch on the drawn line and trim ¼" away from the seam.

Top Cozy Cocoa Handle Unit should measure 1 ½" x 2 ½".

Make one.

With right sides facing, layer a Fabric C square on the right end of a Fabric H rectangle.

Stitch on the drawn line and trim ¼" away from the seam.

Bottom Cozy Cocoa Handle Unit should measure 1 ½" x 2 ½".

Make one.

Assemble Unit.

Cozy Cocoa Handle Unit should measure 2 ½" x 7 ½".

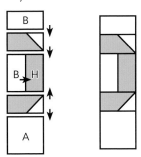

Make one.

Assemble Block.

Cozy Cocoa Block should measure 7 ½" x 7 ½".

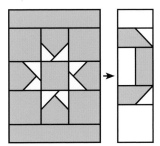

Make one.

67 ½" x 81 ½"

Cutting Instructions:

FROM THE BACKGROUND AND INNER BORDER FABRIC CUT:

1 - 4 ½" x 13 ½" rectangle	A
1 - 3 ¾" x 12 ½" rectangle	B
4 - 3 ½" x 5 ½" rectangles	C
7 - 2 ½" x width of fabric strips	D
3 - 2" x 35 ½" strips	E
1 - 2" x 32" strip	F
1 - 2" x 12 ½" rectangle	G
2 - 1 ¾" x 24 ½" strips	H
1 - 1 ¾" x 12 ½" rectangle	I
2 - 1 ½" x 14 ½" rectangles	J
1 - 1 ½" x 7 ½" rectangle	K
1 - 1 ½" x 5 ½" rectangle	L

FROM THE MIDDLE BORDER FABRIC CUT:

7 - 2 ½" x width of fabric strips — M

FROM THE OUTER BORDER FABRIC CUT:

2 - 6 ½" x 69 ½" length of fabric strips — N
5 - 6 ½" x width of fabric strips — O

FROM THE BINDING FABRIC CUT:

9 - 2 ½" x width of fabric strips — P

Quilt Center:

Assemble Unit.

Top Left Quilt Center Unit should measure 30" x 35 ½".

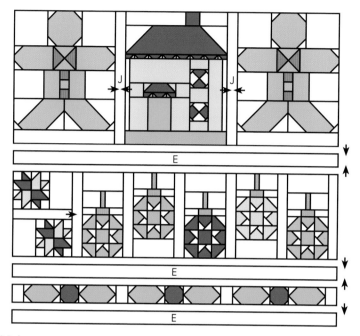

Make one.

Assemble Unit.

Center Quilt Center Unit should measure 18 ½" x 24 ½".

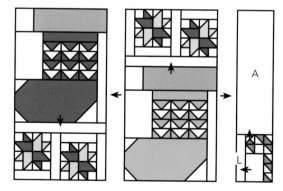

Make one.

Assemble Unit.

Bottom Left Quilt Center Unit should measure 32" x 35 ½".

Make one.

Assemble Unit.

Right Quilt Center Unit should measure 12 ½" x 61 ½".

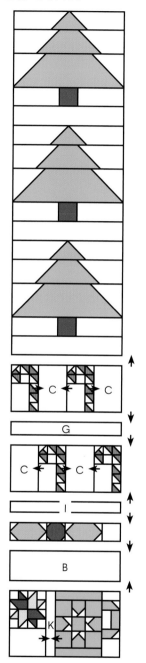

Make one.

Assemble Quilt Center.

Quilt Center should measure 47 ½" x 61 ½".

Inner Border:

Piece the Fabric D strips end to end.

Subcut into:

      2 - 2 ½" x 61 ½" strips (Side Inner Borders - D1)

      2 - 2 ½" x 51 ½" strips (Top and Bottom Inner Borders - D2)

Attach the Side Inner Borders.

Attach the Top and Bottom Inner Borders.

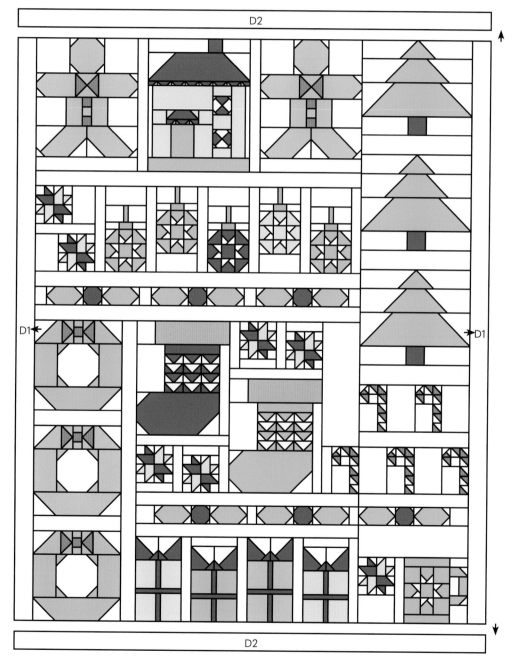

Middle Border:

Piece the Fabric M strips end to end.

Subcut into:

> 2 - 2 ½" x 65 ½" strips (Side Middle Borders - M1)
>
> 2 - 2 ½" x 55 ½" strips (Top and Bottom Middle Borders - M2)

Attach the Side Middle Borders.

Attach the Top and Bottom Middle Borders.

Outer Border:

Piece the Fabric O strips end to end. Pay close attention to direction of fabric when assembling the borders.
Subcut into:

    2 - 6 ½" x 67 ½" strips (Top and Bottom Outer Borders)

Attach side outer borders using the Fabric N strips.

Attach the Top and Bottom Outer Borders.

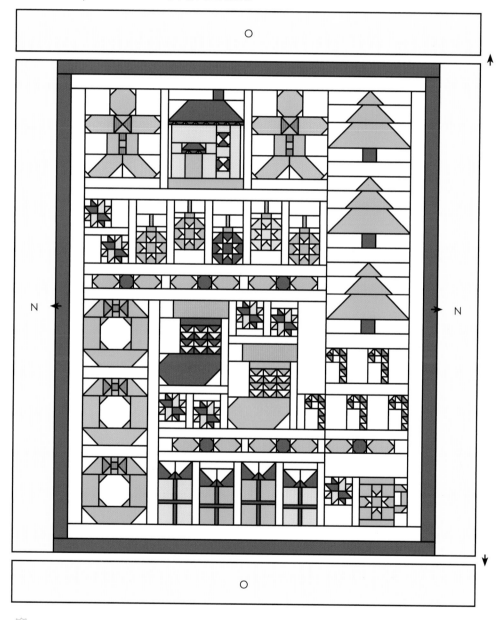

Finishing:

Piece the Fabric P strips end to end for binding.

Quilt and bind as desired.

63" x 63"

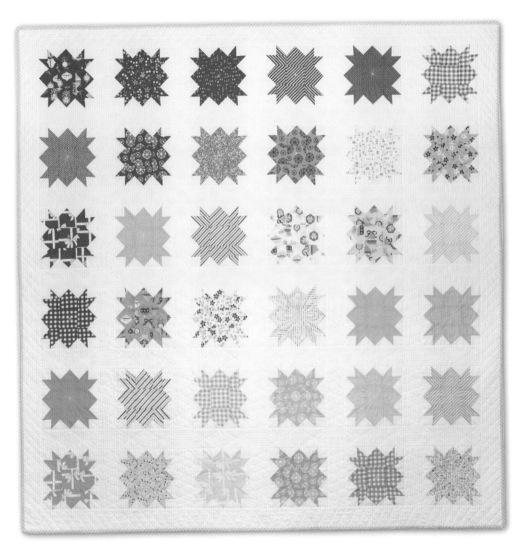

Fabric Requirements:

YARDAGE	DESCRIPTION	FABRICS
3 ½ yards	Background	A to E
36 Fat Eighths	North Star Blocks	F, G & H
¾ yard	Binding	I
4 yards	Backing	

Cutting Instructions:

FROM THE BACKGROUND FABRIC CUT:

72 - 2 ⅛" squares	A
432 - 1 ¾" squares	B
144 - 1 ¾" squares	C
30 - 3" x 8" rectangles	D
15 - 3" x width of fabric strips	E

FROM EACH NORTH STAR BLOCK FABRIC CUT:

5 - 3" squares	F
2 - 2 ⅛" squares	G
4 - 1 ¾" x 3" rectangles	H

FROM THE BINDING FABRIC CUT:

8 - 2 ½" x width of fabric strips	I

North Star Blocks:

Draw a diagonal line on the wrong side of the Fabric A squares.

With right sides facing, layer a Fabric A square with a Fabric G square.

Stitch ¼" from each side of the drawn line.

Cut apart on the marked line.

Half Square Triangle Unit should measure 1 ¾" x 1 ¾".

Make four from each North Star Block Fabric.

Make one hundred forty-four total.

Draw a diagonal line on the wrong side of the Fabric B squares.

With right sides facing, layer a Fabric B square on the left end of a Fabric H rectangle.

Stitch on the drawn line and trim ¼" away from the seam.

Partial North Star Corner Unit should measure 1 ¾" x 3".

Make four from each North Star Block Fabric.

Make one hundred forty-four total.

Assemble Unit using matching fabric.

North Star Corner Unit should measure 3" x 3".

Make four from each North Star Block Fabric.

Make one hundred forty-four total.

With right sides facing, layer a Fabric B square on the top left corner of a Fabric F square.

Stitch on the drawn line and trim ¼" away from the seam.

Repeat on the top right corner.

North Star Point Unit should measure 3" x 3".

Make four from each North Star Block Fabric.

Make one hundred forty-four total.

Assemble Block using matching fabric.

North Star Block should measure 8" x 8".

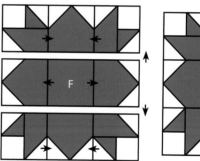 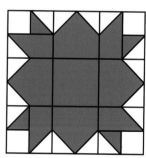

Make one from each North Star Block Fabric.

Make thirty-six total.

Quilt Center:

Piece the Fabric E strips end to end.

Subcut into:

     5 - 3" x 58" strips (Sashing - E1)

     2 - 3" x 58" strips (Side Borders - E2)

     2 - 3" x 63" strips (Top and Bottom Borders - E3)

Assemble Quilt Center. Press toward the sashing.

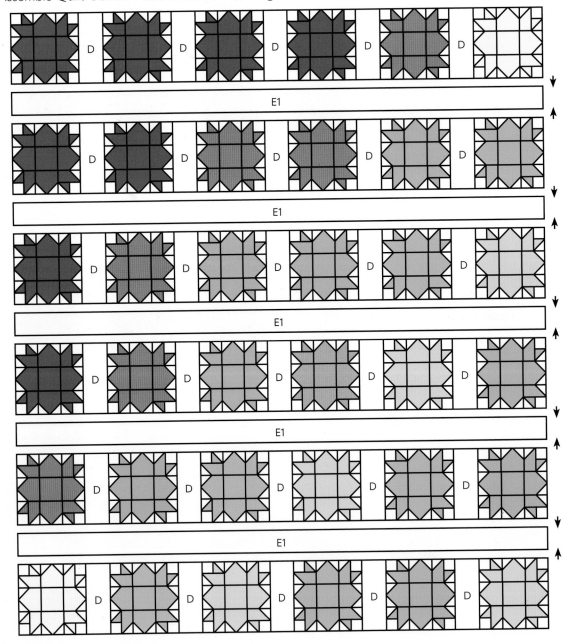